Summer's Coming In

Books for Young People by Natalia Belting

Summer's Coming In
Winter's Eve
Christmas Folk
The Stars Are Silver Reindeer
The Earth Is on a Fish's Back
Calendar Moon
The Sun Is a Golden Earring
Elves and Ellefolk: Tales of Little People
Indy and Mr. Lincoln
Verity Mullens and the Indian
Cat Tales

Summer's Coming In

by NATALIA BELTING

illustrated by Adrienne Adams

HOLT, RINEHART AND WINSTON · New York · Chicago · San Francisco

Text Copyright © 1970 by Natalia Belting.
Illustrations Copyright © 1970 by Adrienne Adams.
All rights reserved, including the right to reproduce
this book or portions thereof in any form.
Published simultaneously in Canada by Holt, Rinehart
and Winston of Canada, Limited.
SBN: 03-084250-6 (Trade)
SBN: 03-084251-4 (HLE)
Library of Congress Catalog Card Number: 74-98921
Printed in the United States of America
First Edition

Title II

Project No.

12-72

*For all the McColleys, and
especially Rebecca, Teresa,
Susanna, Margaret, and Carolyn*

Winter breaks.
Gray banks of fog melt
Into shining jasper cliffs.

The fairies churn up
Buttercups and marigolds,
Bleach elfin linens where
Stone laced with hawthorn
Into hedges rises up the hills
To meet the blue-swept skies.

Blended wine and rose and musk,
The gorse cascades
Into the valleys
And pollarded willows
Cast green shadows
On the streams.

The winds

Brim with sounds of far-off waves

And songs of soaring larks,

Roll tides of incense

From red clover fields

Across cabbage patch

And pasture.

The cuckoo teases softly,
First here and then away,
Nearby and yonder,
                Whispers, calls,
                Cries, summer's coming in.

April 23

St. George's Day
The troops go out,
All the King's men
In scarlet and gold,

All the King's horses,
Ribboned, bedecked.
And the King goes out
In cap of state and crown,

The Lord Mayor in his regalia girt,
The Bishop in silks,
With jeweled staff and ringed gloves.

The guildsmen go out,
Craftsmen, in liveries
Many-hued, like rare fowl;

And the Merchant-Adventurers,
Lords of the Staple,
Aldermen,
Wearing fine stuffs and lace.

On George's Day,
All go out,
> Townsmen,
> Mummers,
>> Hobby the Horse,
>> Tom the Fool,
>> Snap the Dragon.

They all go out,
March through the town,
Down and around,

> Beat out the bounds,
> Make sure the King knows,
> And the Bishop,
> Where the city begins,
> The countryside ends.

On George's Day,
All go out,

Race horse against horse,
Make merry, feast,

For summer's coming in.

At dusk

In the towns,

In April twilight,

The Mayers sing, with fiddle and flute:

    All in this pleasant evening, together comers we,

    For the summer springs so fresh, and green and gay;

    We'll tell you a blossom and buds on every tree,

    Drawing near to the merry month of May.

        Rise up, O master of this house, put on your chain of gold,

        For summer springs so fresh, and green and gay.

        Rise up, O mistress of this house, with gold upon your breast,

        For summer springs so fresh, and green and gay.

        Rise up, O children of this house, all in your rich attire,

        For summer springs so fresh, and green and gay.

    God bless this house and arbor, your riches and your store.

    And now we're going to leave you, in peace and plenty here.

    We shall not sing you May again until another year

    For to draw you these cold winters away.

April 24

St. Mark's Eve
The future's told
All who ask it.
    Young maids
    Stir up a Dumb Cake:
    Unspeaking, mix
          An egg-shell full of salt
          An egg-shell full of malt
          An egg-shell full of barley-meal,

And when the cakes need turning on the fire,
The ones they are to marry
Come without a word,
Turn the cakes,
And go.

Young men
Put nuts in the hot coals,
Give a maiden's name to each,
Wait while the nuts grow hot,

    Saying,
        If you love me, pop and fly,
        If not, lie there silently.

At midnight
The sheeted shapes
Of all who are to die
Before the summer's gone
Or St. Mark's comes again,

Pass through the churchyard,
Wind round the gravestones,
Walk silent past the folk
    Who watch
    Hid in the shadows of the church.

April 30

Beltane night,
    The witches are out
    Riding corn stalks.

        Boggles and bogeys
        Strideleg wild straws,
        Fleet upon mischief.

The gorse is fired,
The high rocks piled with ash wood
    Set ablaze
    To drive the witches out.

Against the goblins
Red thread is tied
In each cow's tail,
And boughs of rowan nailed up in byre and shed.

On Beltane night,
   Till May Day comes,
   With summer,

        Young men and boys,
        Old men too,

                Go out and about
                Raising a din
                With fiddle and fife and drum and horn

                        To drive the elves
                        Back underground.

May 1

Bel fires spiral,
Twist, leap,
Fall, blown dark

    By the May horns' sound,
    The bagpipes swirl,
    The drums beat.

And Hobby the Horse
And Tom the Fool
And Snap the Dragon
        Get the townsfolk up,
        Rouse the sluggards out
                To the near hill
                To see the summer sun rise.
Then
Bannocks, deep-marked
With circle and cross, one to a side,
Are rolled down the hill,

Augurs of death when they rest
Circles uppermost,

Augurs of wealth, long life
When they stop
With crosses atop.

Now the Mayers go out,
The lads,
Up the hills
To fetch the Maypole tree...

Now the Mayers go out, the small ones
To the meadows
Before summer stars fade,
    After fresh blooms
    For May wreaths...

Now the Mayers go out, all the young maids
For
    The one who bathes in dew
    'Neath the hawthorn tree
    The first May day
    Will ever after handsome be.

In the new dawn
The Mayers are out,
Bairns beribboned,
Hoisting long sticks
Top-tufted with marigolds,
Primroses, yarrow.

Down through the streets,
Up through the town
They go singing:
> Gentlemen and ladies
> We wish you a happy May.
> We've come to show our garlands
> Because it is May Day.

> Good morning Master, Mistress,
> We wish you a happy day.
> Please to smell our garlands,
> Because it is the first of May.

May Day
The mummers go out,
   Dressed all in white
   Got up in green,

   Hid behind masks,
   Hideous, fierce.

With ribbons and wreaths
The mummers go out
To dance the long dance,
Threading the Needle
      This way
         And that,

Hands joined,

Back through the lane,
Round by the path,

Thread through the crofts,
Thread through the yards,

Thread the whole town,
Thread to the green
   And the Maypole,

   Dance round the Maypole,
   Singing:

See what a Maypole we have got,
Trit, trit, trot.

Round the Maypole, round we go,
See what a Maypole we can show.

   Round, round, round
   We go,
   Round the Maypole,
   Trit, trit, trot.

May Day

The Queen of Winter comes out
   In fox furs, lamb's wool,
   Hooded in skins,
   Booted.

And all her troops with her,
   In helmets,
   With shields, spears,
   Armed
   With cold and damp.

Then summer's queen comes, the Queen of May,
   In gossamer garb,
   Slippers of sunlight,
            With all her troops
            Kilted and sandaled,
            Bare-armed.

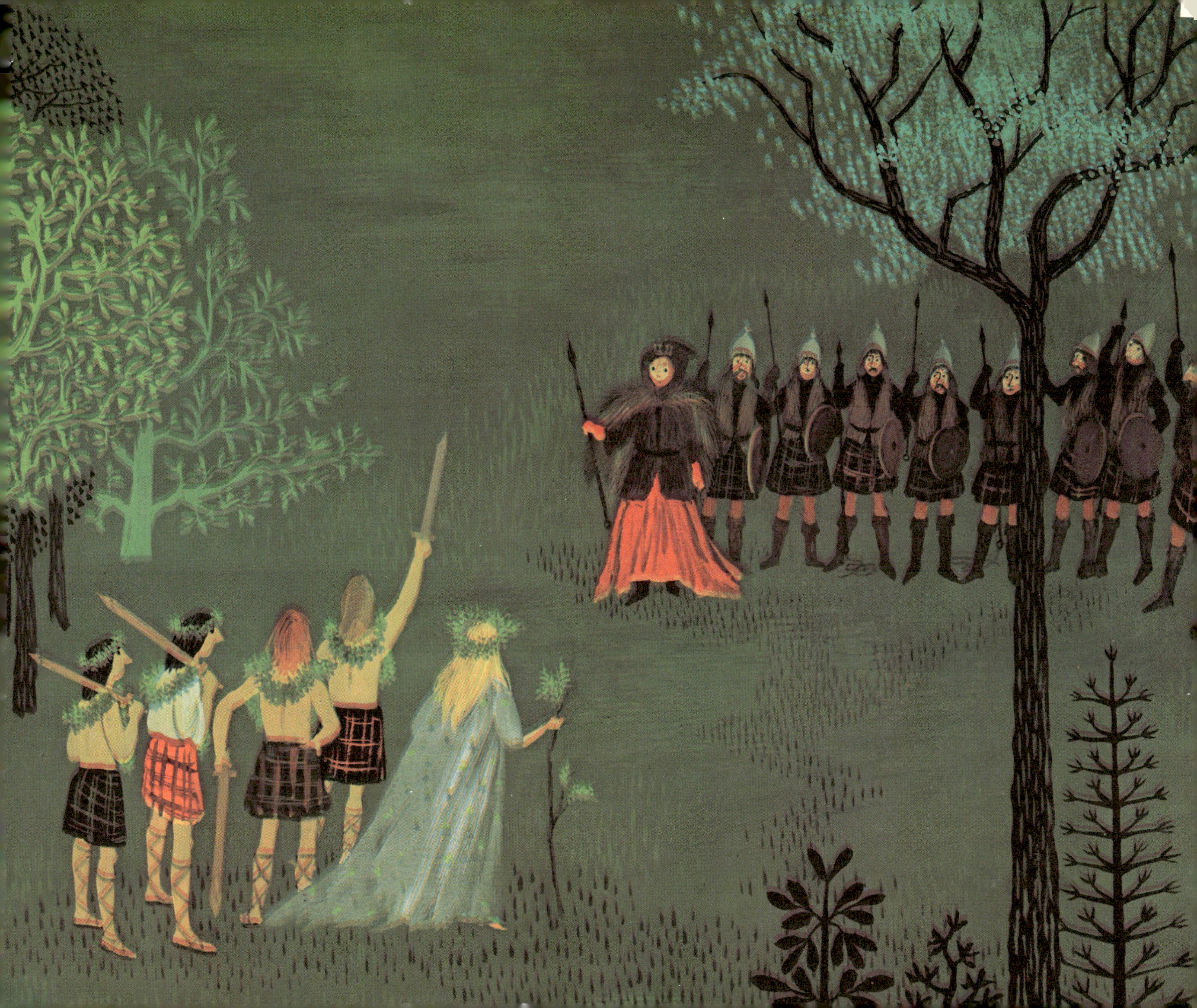

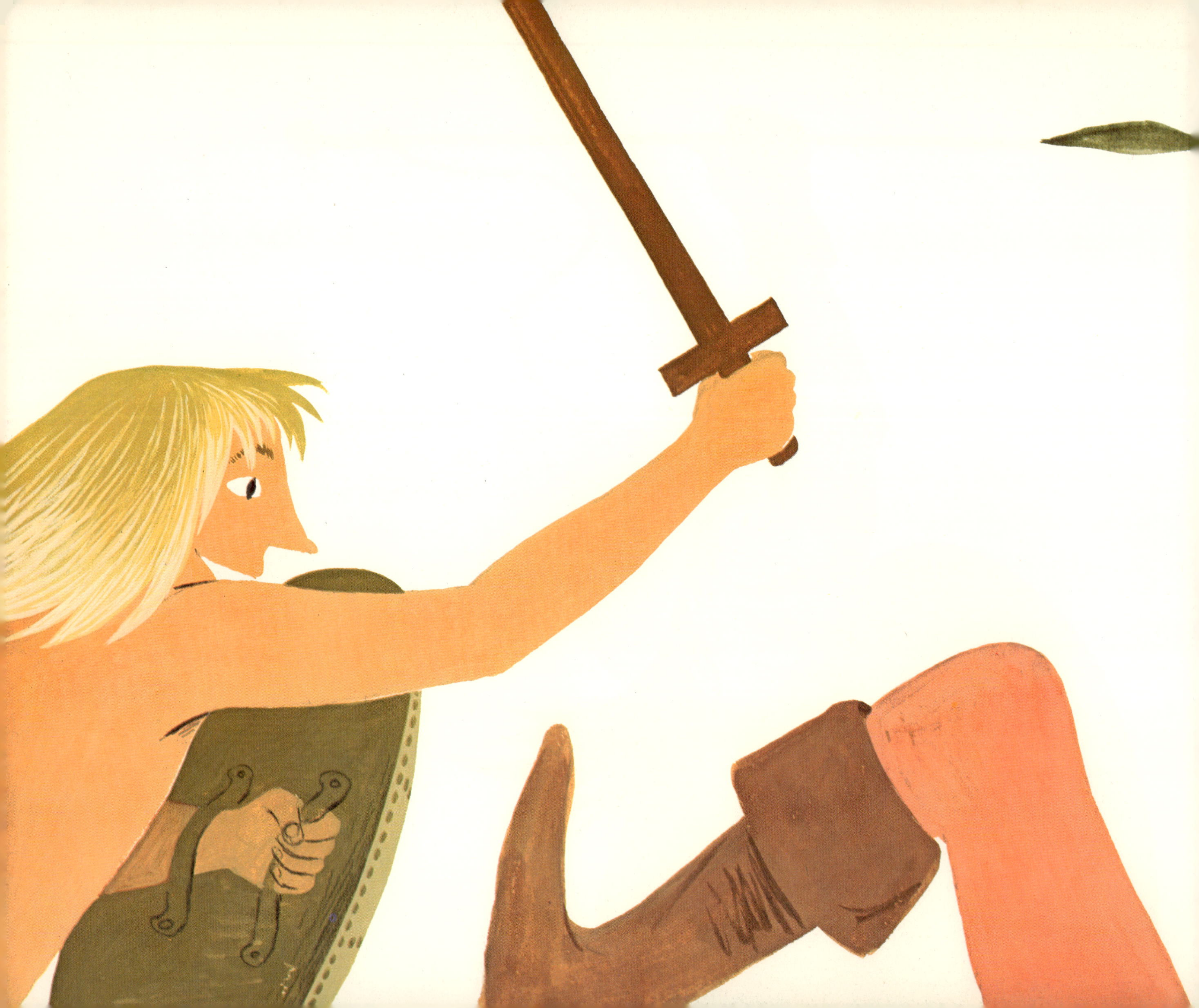

The length of the morning,

The armies battle,

Attack, fall back,

    Cry, winter rules,

    Cry, summer's come to stay.

And if, mischance,

When noon comes,

The troops of summer have not won,

    Then they must ransom

    Their queen's slipper

        With a feast for all the town.

Any of the days,
The first summer days,

Are for visiting the wells,
And the south-running streams,

    To drink,
    To bathe
           All sickness away.
    To open blind eyes,
    Straighten limbs that are bent,
        Cure all the ills
        Demons have brought,
        Guard against those
        They might bring
        Before the next May.

Any of these days,
These May-summer days,

Are for thanking the wells,
And the south-running streams,

Dressing them
With garlands and nosegays,
Bright ribbons and lace
Wove together in hoops

And hung where the waters
Can see the fresh colors,
Breathe the fresh scents.

May 8

Today
Robin Hood and Little John,
Both have come to the fair.

   Little John and Friar Tuck,
   Both have come to the fair.

      Come from the greenwood,
      Come to the fair,

      Come with Maid Marian
      And the merry men.

They all have come to the fair,
Come to the Furry Fair.

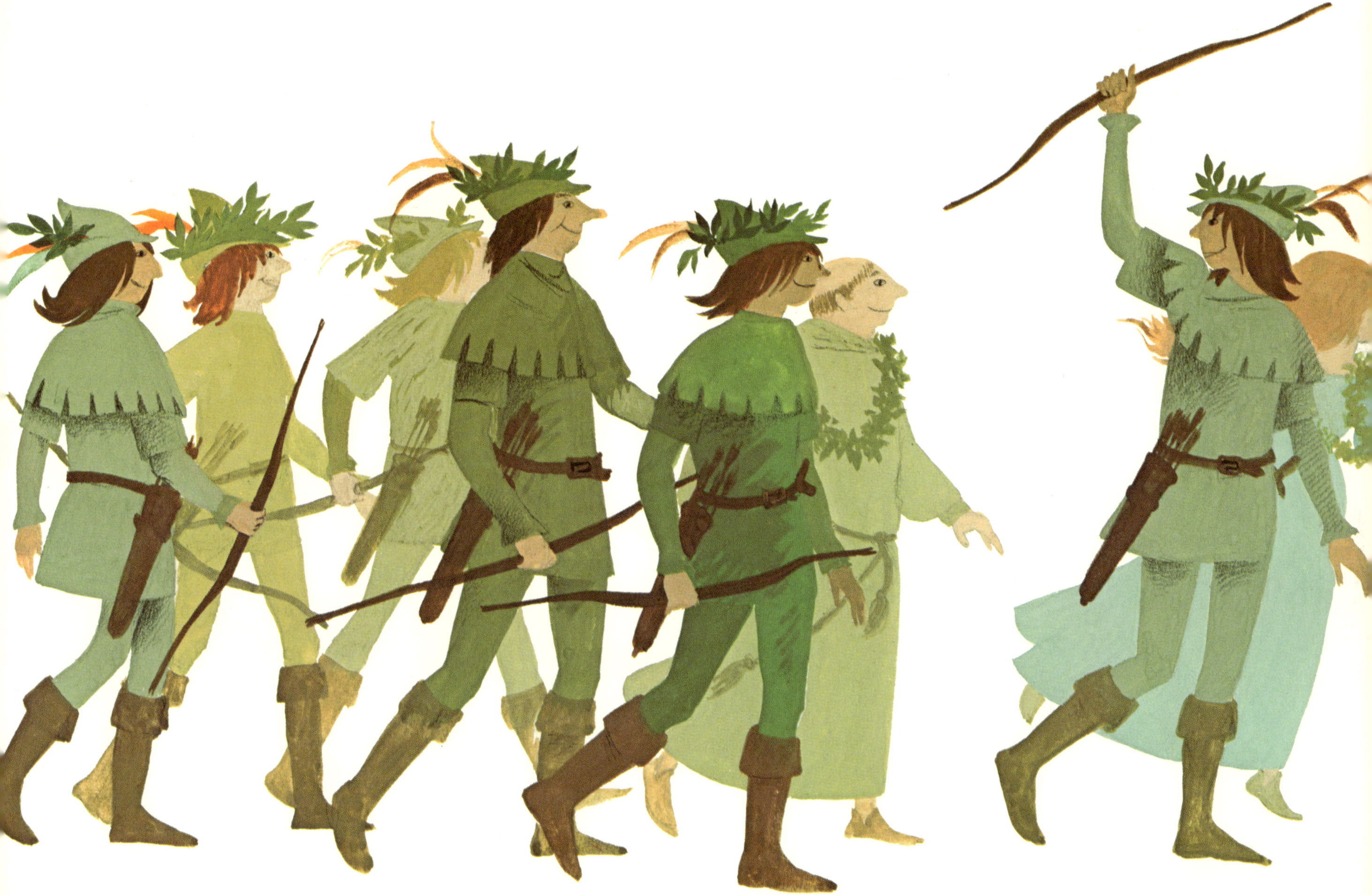

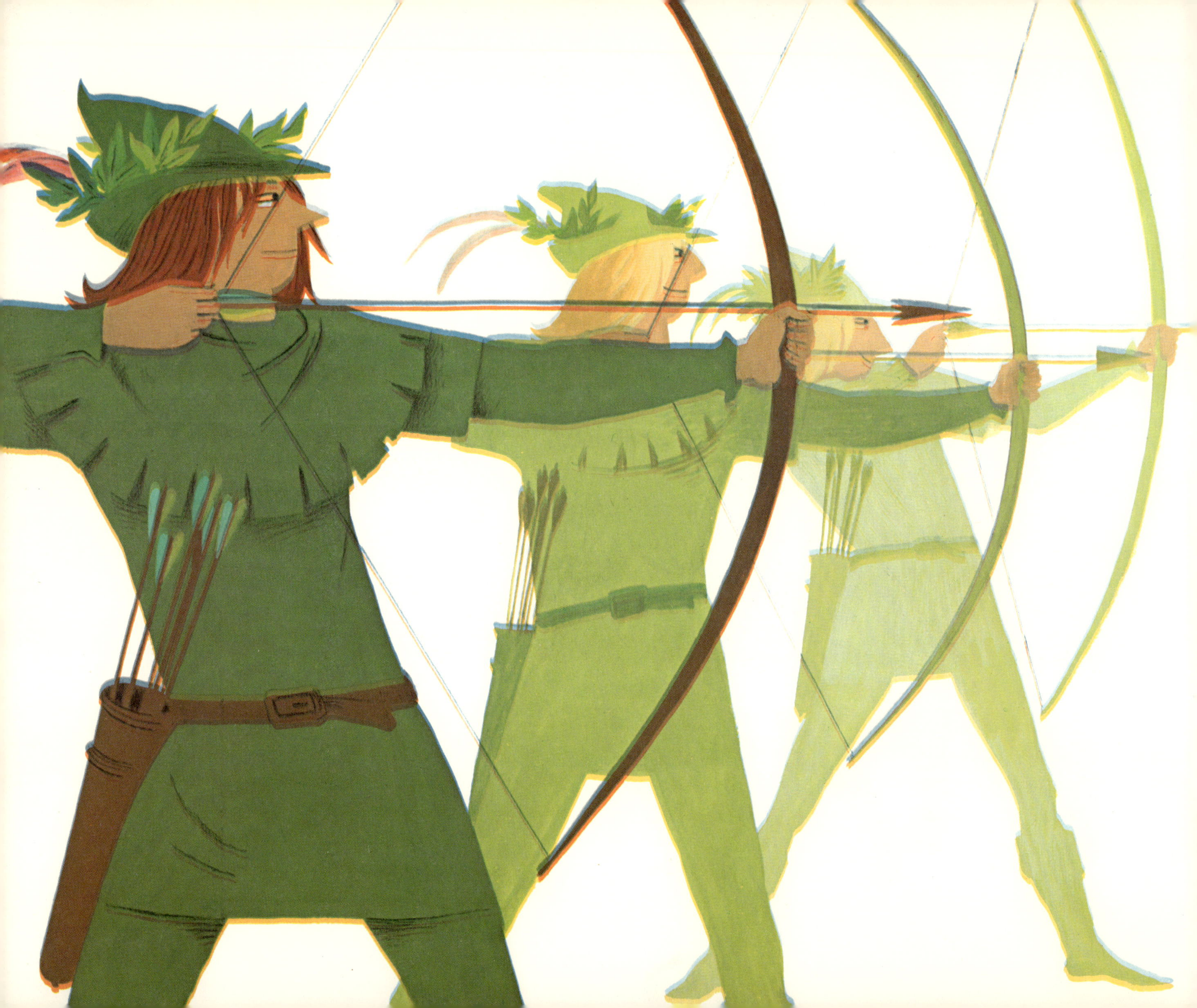

King of the Outlaws,
Robin Hood,

King of the Bowmen,
Robin Hood
Matches his skill
With the best archers round

        At cutting and fashioning
        Arrows that sing

                When they slice from his bow,
                Split arrows on target
                Clean through the hafts.

Little John wins at leaping the stream,
Friar Tuck at eating the spit-roasted pig,

And no maid compares
In fairness and grace

        With Robin Hood's Marian
        This day
        At the Furry Fair.

May 14

The fourteenth of May
Is Gingerbread Day
(Or the first,
Or the tenth,
Or any May day.)

Then Tiddy Doll,
Or Johnny Jack,
   The baker,
     Whatever his name,

Wears a gingerbread hat,
   A great gingerbread hat,
   With a crown so high,
   A brim so wide,
        All gilded and frosted,
          A marvelous, wonderful gingerbread hat.

And townsfolk breakfast,
Even lunch
On gingerbread,
Spicy and hot.

When he has sold
Every bit he has baked,
He tosses his hat,
The gingerbread hat,
Up in the air.

Then everyone round,
  Even Hobby
  And Snap
  And Tom the Fool,

    Scrambles
    To pick up the pieces
    Off the ground.

All the days of May,
The whole of May,
Are for gingerbread,
Fairs,
Frolicking,
Mumming,
For garlands and Maypoles

For now has summer come in.

About the Author Natalia Belting, a historian, has been on the faculty of the University of Illinois since 1941. Combining her knowledge of history and folklore with her poetic style, she has become well known in the field of children's literature. Miss Belting's skill is highlighted in *The Sun Is a Golden Earring*, a runner-up for the Caldecott Medal; *Calendar Moon*, an A.L.A. Notable Book; and her most recent free verse, *Winter's Eve* and *Christmas Folk*. A resident of Urbana, Illinois, she enjoys gardening and cooking in her spare time.

About the Artist Adrienne Adams, born in Arkansas, was educated at Stephens College and the University of Missouri. Her distinguished children's book illustrations have twice made her a runner-up for the Caldecott Medal. She lives on twenty-seven acres of woodland in New Jersey with her husband, author John Anderson. Miss Adams notes, that for *Summer's Coming In*, "I chose casein when I realized that I had a number of night scenes which called for dark, rich color. Caseins are a mixture of water paint and a milk product, which serves as a binder. I like them because they cover well and one can work over and over them, making changes as the picture grows in one's mind."

About the Book The title is hand-lettered and the text typeface is set in Goudy Old Style. The book is printed by offset.